JUST DANCE

Spotlight on Dance Teams

Mel Hammond

Lerner Publications ◆ Minneapolis

Lerner Publications Company
An imprint of Lerner Publishing Group, Inc.
241 First Avenue North
Minneapolis, MN 55401 USA

For reading levels and more information, look up this title at www.lernerbooks.com.

Main body text set in Mikado.
Typeface provided by HVD.

Designer: Mary Ross
Lerner team: Martha Kranes

Library of Congress Cataloging-in-Publication Data

Names: Hammond, Mel, author.
Title: Spotlight on dance teams / Mel Hammond.
Description: Minneapolis, MN : Lerner Publications, [2025] | Series: Just dance (Lerner sports rookie) | Includes bibliographical references and index. | Audience: Ages 5–8 | Audience: Grades K–1 | Summary: "Dive into the exciting world of dance teams. There are different kinds of dance teams, but all feature dancers working together. Young readers learn more about dance teams and what to expect when joining one"—Provided by publisher.
Identifiers: LCCN 2023039504 (print) | LCCN 2023039505 (ebook) | ISBN 9798765625675 (library binding) | ISBN 9798765628843 (paperback) | ISBN 9798765634042 (epub)
Subjects: LCSH: Dance teams—Juvenile literature. | Dance—Juvenile literature.
Classification: LCC GV1798 .H26 2025 (print) | LCC GV1798 (ebook) | DDC 793.3—dc23/eng/20230829

LC record available at https://lccn.loc.gov/2023039504
LC ebook record available at https://lccn.loc.gov/2023039505

Manufactured in the United States of America
1-1010140-51901-1/5/2024

Table of Contents

Chapter 1

Welcome to the Team

Are you and your friends ready to show off your moves? On a dance team, dancers come together to put on a show.

Jewelz

There are many types of dance teams. Some teams do jazz dances. Some perform with pom-poms.

P&G
Kroger
PNC

You can see dance teams at sporting events. Dance teams also perform on TV and in movies.

LAS VEGAS
ACES
LAS VEGAS
ACES

Chapter 2

Getting Ready

Dancers practice in stretchy and loose clothes that let them move. They usually wear jazz shoes or tennis shoes. Dance teams usually perform to upbeat music.

★ Tip ★

Drink water. Dancing is hard work!

You might have to audition to be on a dance team. That means you dance in front of judges. Judges decide who will be on the team.

123
124
147
146

Chapter 3

What to Expect

At practice, the coach teaches everyone a dance move. The team practices it. Then everyone learns another move.

★ Tip ★

It's okay to make a mistake. Keep going!

The team puts all the moves together. They dance to music.

★ Up Close! ★

How to Do a Toe Touch

- Stand on a mat. Hold your arms straight above your head.
- Swing your arms down. Bend your knees.
- Jump!
- Spread your legs wide. Reach for your toes.

Chapter 4

Putting on a Show

Dance teams perform on a stage or at sporting events. Sometimes they compete against other teams.

Everyone on the team wears a uniform. The team shows off the dances they've learned. At competitions, judges give the team a score.

It's fun to dance together. Now it's your turn!

★ Fun Fact ★

Some people create their own dance teams. They perform at home or at talent shows.

Glossary

audition: a dance test to decide who can join a team

competition: an event where teams perform for a prize

uniform: matching clothes that team members wear

Learn More

Clarke, Ginjer L. *A World of Dancers*. New York: Penguin Young Readers, 2023.

Gramson, Hannah. *Spotlight on Hip-Hop.* Minneapolis: Lerner Publications, 2025.

Murray, Julie. *Competitive Dance*. Minneapolis: Abdo Kids, 2023.

Index

Photo Acknowledgments

Image credits: ANDREW CABALLERO-REYNOLDS/AFP via Getty Images, p. 5; Jason Whitman/NurPhoto/Alamy, p. 7; Ethan Miller/Getty Images, p. 9; Jerry Holt/Star Tribune via Getty Images, p. 11; Mike Maple/The Commercial Appeal/ZUMAPRESS.com via Alamy, p. 13; FatCamera/Getty Images, p. 15; Westend61/Getty Images, p. 17; Joseph Calomeni/Getty Images, p. 19; Ray Evans/Alamy, p. 21; Ian Allenden/Alamy, p. 23. Design elements: Kilroy79/Getty Images, Iuliia Mashinets/Getty Images.

Cover: Christian Gooden/Tribune Content Agency LLC/Alamy.